Fact Finders®

WHAT YOU NEED TO KNOW ABOUT
DIABETES

BY AMANDA PETERSON

CONSULTANT:
MARJORIE J. HOGAN, MD
UNIVERSITY OF MINNESOTA
AND HENNEPIN COUNTY MEDICAL CENTER
ASSOCIATE PROFESSOR OF PEDIATRICS
AND PEDIATRICIAN

CAPSTONE PRESS
a capstone imprint

Fact Finders Books are published by Capstone Press,
1710 Roe Crest Drive, North Mankato, Minnesota 56003
www.capstonepub.com

Library of Congress Cataloging-in-Publication Data
Cataloging-in-Publication data is on file with the Library of Congress.
ISBN 978-1-4914-4833-5 (library binding)
ISBN 978-1-4914-4901-1 (paperback)
ISBN 978-1-4914-4919-6 (eBook PDF)

Developed and Produced by Focus Strategic Communications, Inc.
Adrianna Edwards: project manager
Ron Edwards: editor
Rob Scanlan: designer and compositor
Mary Rose MacLachlan: media researcher
Francine Geraci: copy editor and proofreader
Wendy Scavuzzo: fact checker

Photo Credits
Alamy: Phanie, 15; Amanda Peterson, 14; iStockphoto: bjones27, 26, leonello, 7; Massachusetts General Hospital Diabetes Research Center, 27; Science Source, 9 (left), BSIP, 6, Jim Varney, 25, RIA Novosti, 24, Richard T. Nowitz, 28; Shutterstock: Africa Studio, 10 (bottom), Aleksandrs Samuilovs, 23 (middle left), Alexander Raths, 18, Alila Medical Media, 13, 16, 17, Anetta, 4 (left), antoniodiaz, 22 (left), Bochkarev Photography, 5, Bryan Solomon, 23 (left), Dmitry Lobanov, 22 (right), doraclub, 21, everything possible (background), back cover and throughout, Kalin Eftimov, 23 (middle), Kletr, 10 (top), M. Unal Ozmen, 23 (right), Michael D. Brown, 12, Olga Zaretska, 4 (right), Ondrej83, 20, ratmaner, cover (bottom), 1 (back) and throughout, Sergey Novikov, 29, Sherry Yates Young, 19, Valentina Razumova, 23 (middle right), Vasilis Ververidis, cover (top); University of Toronto Archives, 8, 9 (right)

Printed in China
042015   008831LEOF15

TABLE OF CONTENTS

CHAPTER 1
WHAT IS DIABETES?

Something was wrong with 7-year-old Noah. Suddenly he was always tired. He even fell asleep at a baseball game. He complained of being thirsty. And he started making frequent trips to the bathroom. Noah's parents took him to the doctor. They were surprised to learn he had lost 7 pounds (3 kilograms) in just a few months. His blood sugar level was over 600. That's many times higher than normal! Noah was admitted to a hospital. There, doctors confirmed he had a **disease** called type 1 diabetes. He would have it his entire life.

Noah stayed in the hospital for several days. He learned that his body had trouble using a special kind of sugar called **glucose**. Without it his organs could not work properly.

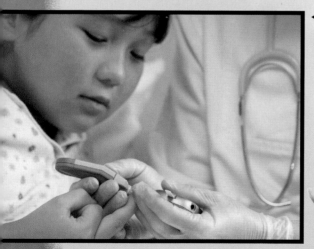

◀ Patients with diabetes prick their fingers to get blood samples. The blood samples are used to determine blood sugar levels.

blood glucose meter ▶

4

Doctors taught Noah and his family how to monitor his blood sugar. In one day Noah had to prick his finger around eight times! They also showed him how to inject **insulin** into his body. Insulin helps cells use glucose. Soon Noah was acting like himself again. His diabetes would never go away. But it also would not stop him from living an active life.

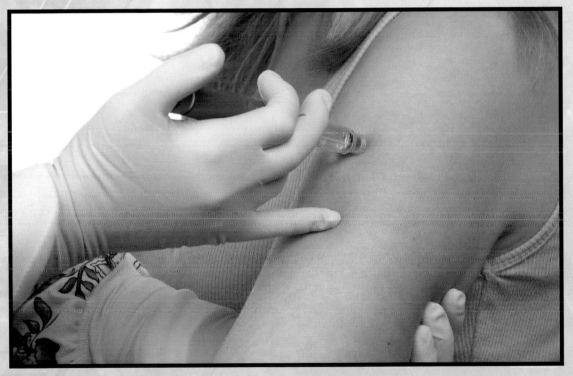

▲ insulin injection

disease—a sickness or illness

glucose—a natural sugar found in plants that gives energy to living things

insulin—a substance made in the pancreas that helps the body use sugar

INSULIN AND DIABETES

When you eat, your body changes some of the food into a sugar. This sugar is known as glucose. It enters your blood. Then a **hormone** called insulin is released. Your cells open up and absorb the glucose. Your cells change the glucose into energy. This is the sugar cycle. Your body needs energy for everything from thinking to playing. Glucose can also be stored for later use.

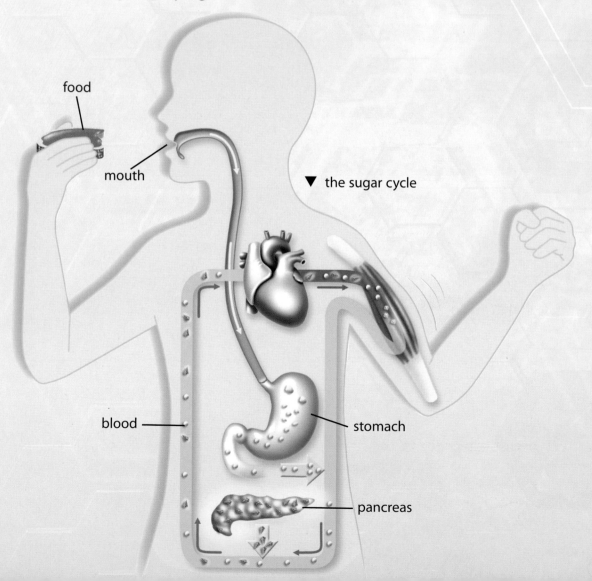

food

mouth

▼ the sugar cycle

blood

stomach

pancreas

Sometimes the **pancreas** does not make enough insulin. Sometimes the body cannot use insulin. If the body cannot absorb glucose, it will build up in the blood. That can result in diabetes. This disease could cause damage to organs such as the heart or kidney. It could even result in death.

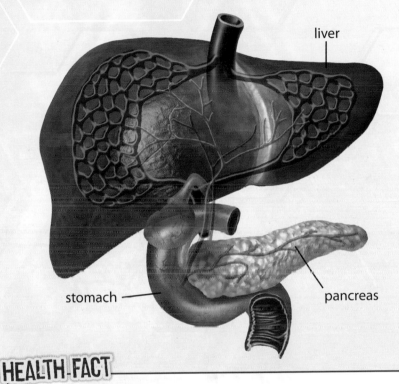

liver

stomach

pancreas

HEALTH FACT

The pancreas is located near the stomach. Most people don't think much about it until a problem occurs. When cells in the pancreas are damaged, diabetes can result.

hormone—a chemical made by a gland in the body that affects a person's growth and development

pancreas—an organ near the stomach that makes insulin

HISTORY OF DIABETES

The first people to describe diabetes were the ancient Egyptians more than 3,000 years ago. For many years people showed signs of this disease. They were tired and thirsty. But no one knew how to help them. In 1776 Dr. Matthew Dobson proved that diabetics had extra sugar in their blood and urine. Then in 1889, scientists wanted to understand the role of the pancreas in digestion. They removed a pancreas from a dog. The animal developed diabetes.

In 1921 doctors Frederick Banting and Charles Best made a huge discovery. They learned that insulin from a cow's pancreas could be used to treat diabetes. Because of that, millions of people can live long and healthy lives.

▲ Dr. Frederick Banting (right) and his assistant, Dr. Charles Best, with one of the first diabetic dogs saved with insulin

HEALTH FACT

Working as a "water" taster might sound like an easy job. But at one time, it was a gross way to make a living. Water tasters drank other people's urine to see if it was sugary. A person whose urine tasted sweet was diagnosed as diabetic.

WONDER DRUG

Diabetes had taken over 14-year-old Leonard Thompson's body. Doctors told Leonard's family they could try using insulin from a cow's pancreas to help him. This had never been tried before. But there was no other way to save Leonard's life.

On January 11, 1922, Leonard became the first patient to receive insulin. His blood sugar dropped a little. Twelve days later, doctors gave him insulin that was more pure. It worked. Leonard recovered. With the help of insulin, he lived until 1935.

▼ Leonard Thompson as a boy, before insulin treatment

▼ Leonard Thompson, shown here as an adult, lived to age 27.

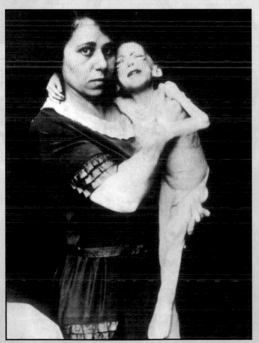

A GROWING PROBLEM

There is a good chance you know someone who has diabetes. Most people who are diabetic are adults. But more and more children are getting the disease. Some experts think that there is a link between being overweight and getting diabetes.

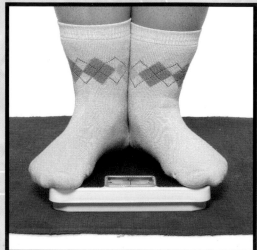

▲ More and more children are overweight.

The number of children who are overweight is growing. Overeating junk food and not getting enough exercise are making kids too heavy. The more time kids spend in front of a TV or video screen, the more likely they are to be overweight.

▼ Inactivity can lead to weight gain.

A GLOBAL CONCERN

Diabetes affects 387 million people around the world. By 2035 there may be nearly 600 million people with this disease.

The number of people worldwide living with diabetes in 2013, according to the International Diabetes Federation

WESTERN PACIFIC — 138 million

SOUTHEAST ASIA — 75 million

EUROPE — 52 million

NORTH AMERICA AND CARIBBEAN — 39 million

MIDDLE EAST AND NORTH AFRICA — 37 million

SOUTH AND CENTRAL AMERICA — 25 million

AFRICA — 22 million

HEALTH FACT

The International Diabetes Federation (IDF) estimates that a person dies from diabetes every 6 seconds. Diabetes was the cause of 1.5 million deaths worldwide in 2013.

CHAPTER 2
TYPES OF DIABETES

There are two main types of diabetes—type 1 and type 2. Type 1 was once known as juvenile diabetes. That is because most people who have it are under the age of 20. In the United States, about 80 percent of kids with diabetes have type 1. But only 5 percent of all diabetics have type 1.

▼ percentage of kids with type 1 and type 2 diabetes in the United States

80 percent type 1

20 percent type 2

HEALTH FACT

Type 1 diabetes has nothing to do with your lifestyle or what you eat. There is nothing you can do to prevent getting it. Currently there is nothing you can do to cure it.

TYPE 1

Type 1 diabetes is a disease of the **immune system**. This is the system that fights off illness. But sometimes it does not work properly. Then it attacks healthy cells.

Scientists are not sure why this happens. A **virus** might trigger the start of the disease. As the immune system fights the virus, it might create **antibodies**. These substances cannot tell the difference between virus cells and healthy cells. So they may attack both.

In type 1 diabetes, the immune system attacks the pancreas. It fights the healthy cells that create insulin. Eventually the pancreas will make little or no insulin. This means the body does not get the insulin it needs.

▼ Type 1 diabetes can damage body organs and tissue.

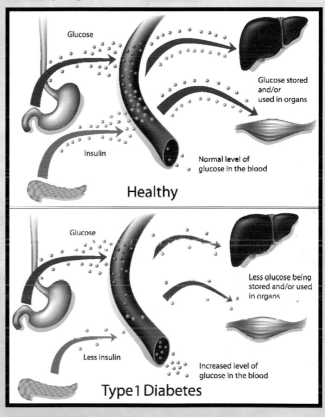

immune system—the part of the body that protects against germs and diseases

virus—a germ that infects living things and causes diseases

antibody—a substance in the body that fights against infection and disease

13

MEET MOLLY

Nine-year-old Molly held an orange in one hand. In the other she had an insulin-filled shot. She poked the needle through the orange's skin. It was only practice. She had just learned how to test her blood sugar. Insulin injections were the next lesson. She would need to give herself five a day, or nearly 2,000 a year.

Now Molly rarely uses shots, because she has an insulin pump. The small device clips to her pants. A small tube and needle connect the pump to her stomach. After Molly checks her blood sugar levels, she pushes a few buttons on the pump. This tells how much insulin she needs. The pump automatically delivers the correct dose.

Molly is very careful about her diabetes. She tests her blood sugar often. She watches what she eats. Exercise is also an important part of her day. Being diagnosed with type 1 diabetes was scary at first. But Molly learned how to cope with her disease and be healthy. Being diabetic has not stopped her from reaching any of her goals.

insulin pump

▲ Molly with her insulin pump

INSULIN PUMP

A diabetic needs to measure and keep blood sugar at the right level. One way to do this is by using an insulin pump. This small machine sends insulin directly into the body. Small amounts of insulin are sent throughout the day. Diabetics need more insulin when eating. After checking the blood sugar level, the diabetic presses a few buttons on the pump. This tells the machine how much more insulin is needed. An insulin pump is handy. It allows a diabetic to carry on with activities without having to stop all the time to measure glucose levels.

▼ insulin pump

TYPE 2 DIABETES

Type 2 diabetes was once known as adult-onset diabetes. Most people diagnosed with this illness are older than 20. But more and more children and teens are developing this disease. About 22 percent of kids with diabetes have type 2.

Type 2 diabetes is not a disease of the immune system. Several things might cause a person to develop type 2 diabetes. The pancreas may not produce enough insulin. Or the person's cells may stop absorbing insulin. For some people, both things might happen.

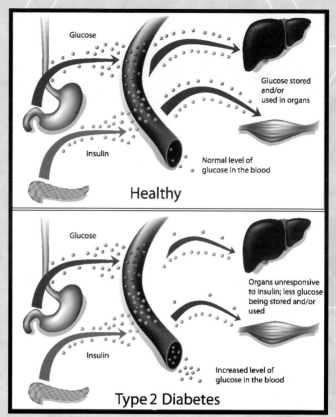

▲ Like type 1 diabetes, type 2 can also cause damage to many different organs, such as the nerves, blood vessels, eyes, and kidneys.

Type 2 diabetes can often be prevented. Most people who are diagnosed with type 2 diabetes are overweight. A healthy diet and regular exercise may help prevent type 2 diabetes.

COMPARING TYPE 1 AND TYPE 2 DIABETES

Type 1	Type 2
usually diagnosed in children	usually diagnosed in adults (although more children are being diagnosed with type 2)
pancreas does not make insulin	pancreas does not make insulin or cells cannot effectively absorb insulin
Symptoms come on suddenly and might include extreme hunger and thirst, rapid weight loss, frequent urination, vomiting, mood changes, tiredness, blurry vision, wounds that heal slowly, and fruity-smelling breath.	Symptoms develop slowly; some type 2 diabetics might not have any symptoms. Factors for getting the disease may include obesity, age, family history, ethnicity, poor diet, and little physical activity.
can be genetic	can be genetic
cannot be prevented	can be prevented
not linked to obesity	linked to obesity
must take insulin	usually no insulin

▶ A healthy pancreas makes insulin, and the body uses it to let glucose into the blood.

▶ In type 1 diabetes, the pancreas doesn't make insulin.

▶ In type 2 diabetes, the pancreas makes insulin, but the body cannot use it.

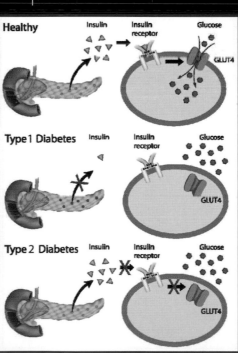

CHAPTER 3
LIVING WITH DIABETES

Kids with diabetes must follow their doctors' advice. Most diabetics have personal plans that help them manage their disease. Things such as glucose monitoring, insulin shots, diabetes pills, a healthy diet, and exercise should be part of a plan to manage diabetes.

▲ People with diabetes should talk with their doctors about plans to manage the disease.

GLUCOSE MONITORING

The best way diabetics can stay on track is to check glucose levels regularly. A blood glucose monitor tests the levels. A special test strip is placed in the machine before each use. Then a finger is pricked, and one drop of blood is placed on the test strip. Seconds later the machine gives a blood glucose level or number. Usually a child's blood sugar is considered normal if it is between 70 and 120. However each person has his or her own range. If the number is high, there is too much sugar in the blood. Insulin will help lower the blood glucose number. If the number is low, there is not enough sugar in the blood. A sugary snack will help raise the number. A very high or low number might mean a trip to the hospital.

▼ blood glucose monitoring kit and insulin

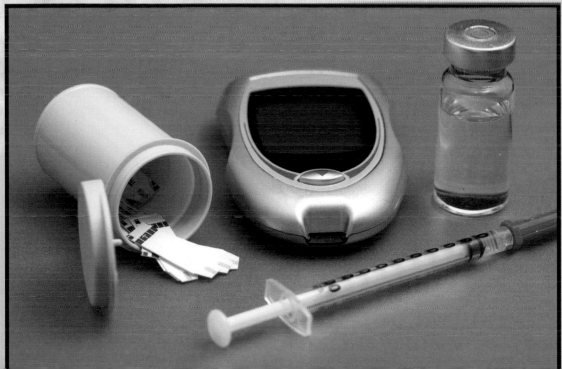

INSULIN SHOTS

Type 1 diabetics must use insulin. Some type 2 diabetics also use insulin. Most diabetics need to use insulin several times a day. Insulin cannot be swallowed. It must be injected into the body. Shots and special insulin pumps put insulin directly into the bloodstream. They are the best ways of taking the drug.

INSULIN PENS

Insulin pens can be used instead of needles and vials. They inject insulin into the blood to regulate the blood sugar levels. They are easy to use. First, click in a new pen needle. Set the dial to the amount of insulin needed. Stick the needle into the skin, and press the button at the end of the pen. The pre-measured cartridges allow accurate dosages with little effort.

▼ insulin pen

HEALTH FACT

Two-thirds of all insulin prescriptions in Europe and Japan are for insulin pens. In the United States, only 15 percent of diabetics use the pen.

DIABETES PILLS

Diabetic pills work only for diabetics who still produce some insulin—the majority of type 2 people. These diabetics take pills to help control their blood sugar. There are different pills for different problems. Some pills help the pancreas make insulin. Others help cells absorb insulin. Diabetics might also take pills that change the way the body absorbs **carbohydrates**. Carbohydrates are the sugars that become glucose. They increase blood sugar levels.

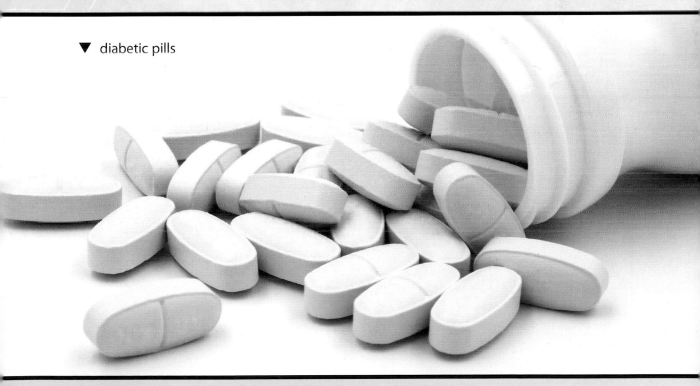

▼ diabetic pills

carbohydrate—a substance found in foods such as bread, rice, cereal, and potatoes that gives you energy

HEALTHY DIET AND EXERCISE

Diabetics should follow a healthy diet. They should eat lots of fruits and vegetables, low-fat dairy products, lean meat, and whole grains. They should avoid fried foods, sugary snacks and sodas, and processed foods.

"Carb counting" can help diabetics keep their blood glucose at the right level. Labels on food and drinks show the number of grams of carbohydrates per serving. Children 5 through 12 should have between 45 and 60 grams of carbohydrates at each meal. Children older than 12 should usually have between 45 and 75 grams at each meal.

◀ looking at nutrition labels

▼ Eating healthy food will help keep your blood glucose at the proper level.

Many diabetics also use the glycemic index (GI) to see what they should and should not eat. This index uses numbers that rank foods by how they affect blood sugar. Foods that have a high GI will raise blood sugar more than foods with a low GI. Many fruits and vegetables are low on the index. White breads and starchy foods, such as potatoes, have high GIs.

Glycemic Index Chart

Low glycemic is 55 or below
High glycemic is 70 or higher

Snacks	GI	Starch	GI	Vegetables	GI	Fruit	GI	Dairy	GI
pizza	33	bagel, plain	33	broccoli	10	cherries	22	yogurt, plain	14
chocolate bar	49	white rice	38	cabbage	10	apples	34	yogurt, low fat	14
potato chips	51	white spaghetti	32	lettuce	10	oranges	40	whole milk	30
popcorn	55	sweet potato	48	mushrooms	10	grapes	43	skim milk	32
blueberry muffin	59	white long grain rice	50	tomatoes	15	kiwis	47	yogurt, fruit	33
soda	65	baked potato	60	green beans	15	bananas	58	chocolate milk	42
doughnut	76	taco shells	68	carrots	41	pineapples	66	custard	43
rice cakes	82	french fries	75	beets	64	watermelons	80	soy milk	44
pretzels	83	instant white rice	87	parsnips	97	dates	103	ice cream	62

SUPPORT IN MANAGING DIABETES

Managing diabetes is hard. Diabetics often need support. Family members and friends can help. So can doctors and school nurses.

▲ diabetes support group

DIABETES AT SCHOOL

A student with diabetes may visit the school nurse for glucose checks. If the number is high, the student might take insulin. If it is low, he or she might have a snack. The student might stay in the nurse's office for a bit and then recheck the number. Once the number is good, the student can rejoin the class.

The school nurse stays in contact with a diabetic student's family, doctor, and teachers. That way, when the student needs support, the nurse will know how to help.

▼ School nurses can help students with diabetes.

CHAPTER 4

THE FUTURE OF DIABETES

More and more people are diagnosed with diabetes. This is a cause for concern. The disease can cost a lot to manage. If not treated, it can keep people from working, being active, and living healthy lives.

◀ Getting treatment for diabetes will help you to live an active life.

HEALTH FACT

In the late 1800s, a child diagnosed with type 1 diabetes might live less than one year. Today type 1 diabetics live long and full lives.

BIONIC PANCREAS

Exciting new technologies will help diabetics manage their disease. For example, scientists have created a **bionic** pancreas. A monitor is attached. It measures glucose levels and sends the information to a smartphone. Samples are taken every 5 minutes. The smartphone figures out how much medicine the body needs. It tells an insulin pump how much medicine to put in the body. The bionic pancreas is still being tested. It is not yet available to the public.

▼ a bionic pancreas

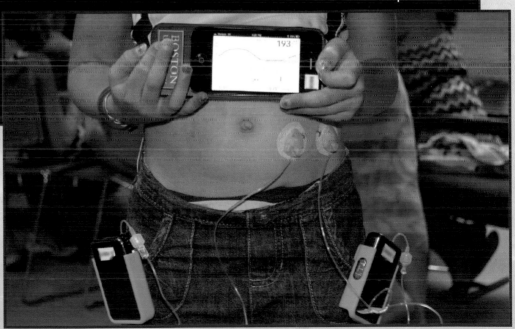

bionic—using mechanical or electronic parts to help humans perform tasks

FINDING A CURE

Around the world, researchers and doctors are working to find a cure for diabetes. Some are studying blood and tissues. They hope this will help them predict if a person will develop type 1 diabetes. If doctors know a patient may become diabetic, they can prescribe medicine to protect the cells that make insulin. This might slow the disease or even keep it from happening.

▼ diabetes research

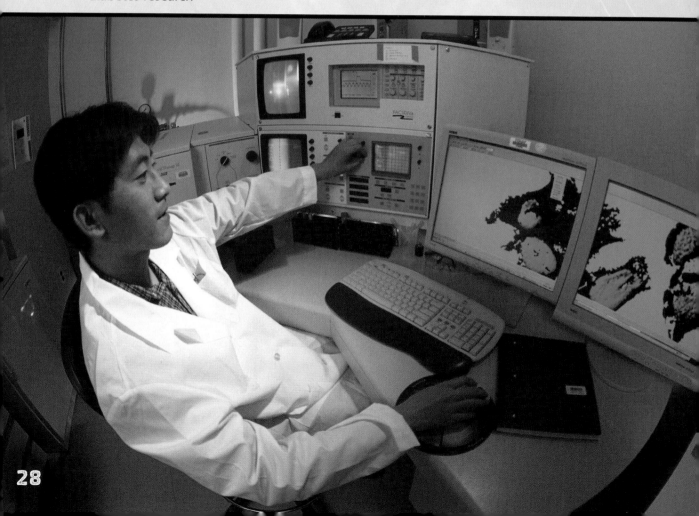

Other scientists have developed cells that make insulin in the pancreas. This is very exciting! Scientists know how to create healthy cells. But they must still figure out how to keep those cells healthy after they are **transplanted**. They want to make sure the diabetic's immune system does not attack the new cells. And they will need a lot of them. Each transplant requires over 150 million cells!

Scientists have been able to cure diabetes in mice. Someday they will be able to cure diabetes in humans too. Better yet, they might discover how to prevent diabetes in the first place!

◀ Diabetes could be cured in the future.

transplant—to transfer organs, tissues, or cells into a body

GLOSSARY

antibody (AN-ti-bah-dee)—a substance in the body that fights against infection and disease

bionic (bye-ON-ik)—using mechanical or electronic parts to help humans perform tasks

carbohydrate (kar-boh-HYE-drate)—a substance found in foods such as bread, rice, cereal, and potatoes that gives you energy

disease (di-ZEEZ)—a sickness or illness

glucose (GLOO-kose)—a natural sugar found in plants that gives energy to living things

hormone (HOR-mohn)—a chemical made by a gland in the body that affects a person's growth and development

immune system (i-MYOON SISS-tuhm)—the part of the body that protects against germs and diseases

insulin (IN-suh-luhn)—a substance made in the pancreas that helps the body use sugar

pancreas (PAN-kree-uhss)—an organ near the stomach that makes insulin

transplant (TRANS-plant)—to transfer organs, tissues, or cells into a body

virus (VYE-ruhss)—a germ that infects living things and causes diseases

READ MORE

Amsel, Sheri. *The Everything Kids' Human Body Book: All You Need to Know About Your Body Systems—From Head to Toe!* Avon, Mass.: Adams Media Corp., 2012.

Chilman-Blair, Kim, and John Taddeo. *What's Up with Ella?: Medikidz Explain Diabetes*. New York: Rosen Publishing's Rosen Central, 2010.

Deland, M. Maitland. *The Great Katie Kate Discusses Diabetes*. Austin, Texas: Greenleaf Books Group Press, 2010.

Kajander, Rebecca. *Be Fit, Be Strong, Be You*. Be the Boss of Your Body. Minneapolis: Free Press Pub., 2010.

Wilsdon, Christina, Patricia Daniels, and Jen Agresta. *Ultimate Bodypedia: An Amazing Inside-Out Tour of the Human Body*. Washington, D.C.: National Geographic Society, 2014.

INTERNET SITES

FactHound offers a safe, fun way to find Internet sites related to this book. All of the sites on FactHound have been researched by our staff.

Here's all you do:

Visit *www.facthound.com*

Type in this code: 9781491448335

 Check out projects, games and lots more at
www.capstonekids.com

INDEX